Our Planet in Peril

Acid Rain

Louise Petheram

Bridgestone Books
an imprint of Capstone Press
Mankato, Minnesota

Originally published as Acid Rain, ©2002 Franklin Watts, United Kingdom

Bridgestone Books are published by Capstone Press
151 Good Counsel Drive, P.O. Box 669, Mankato, MN 56002
http://www.capstone-press.com

Library of Congress Cataloging-in-Publication Data

Petheram, Louise.
   Acid rain / by Louise Petheram.
      v. cm. -- (Our planet in peril)
Includes bibliographical references and index.
Contents: The present situation -- What is acid rain? -- Measuring acid
rain -- What causes acid rain? -- Why are non-industrial areas affected?
-- Threat to human health -- Threat to forests -- Threat to water life
-- Threat to agricultural crops -- Damage to buildings -- The picture
around the world -- The solution so far -- What about the future?
   ISBN 0-7368-1360-8 (hardcover)
  1. Acid rain--Environmental aspects--Juvenile literature. [1. Acid
rain--Environmental aspects. 2. Air--Pollution. 3. Pollution.] I.
Title. II. Series.
   TD195.44 .P48 2003
   363.738'6--dc21

                                          2002009822

Editor: Kate Banham   Illustration: Ian Thompson
Designer: Mark Mills   Picture Research: Diana Morris
Art Direction: Jonathan Hair   Consultant: Sally Morgan, Ecoscene

Photo acknowledgements
The publishers would like to thank the following for their permission to reproduce photographs
in this book.

Greg Abel/Environmental Images: 9bl; Martin Bond/Environmental Images: 28t; Andrew
Brown/Ecoscene: 9t, 17t; Graham Burns/Environmental Images: 11br; John Corbett/Ecoscene:
12t; Corbis: 23t; Colin Cuthbert/SPL: 8t; Stephen Dalton/NHPA: 19t; EPA/Lake Michigan
Federation: fr cover, 22b; Mark Edwards/Still Pictures: 6t, 19b; Mary Evans PL: 10b; Mark
Fallander/Environmental Images: 14cl; © FSC: 17b; Dylan Garcia/Still Pictures: 27b; City of
Tempe, AZ/Diane Bartsch: 15t; Nick Hawkes/Ecoscene: 14tr; Mike Jackson/Still Pictures: 5tl;
Index Stock/Arnie Rosner: 14-15b; Yoram Lehmann/Still Pictures: 11ltr; Charlotte
MacPherson/Environmental Images: 16b; Chris Martin/Environmental Images: 4c; Rick
Miller/Agstock/SPL: 20-21; Sally Morgan/Ecoscene: 17c; U.S. House of Representatives/Energy
and Commerce Committee: 11bl; Juan Carlos Munoz/Still Pictures: 7t; Trevor
Perry/Environmental Images: 12-13b, 21bl; Skjold Photograph 29C; Ray Pforter/ Still Pictures:
22tl; Richard Pike/Still Pictures: 26b; Charlie Pye-Smith: 28-29; Harmut Schwarz/Still Pictures:
23c; R. Sorensen & J.Olsen/NHPA: 18t; Tek Image/SPL: 25t; Wolk-UNEP/Still Pictures: 4-5b.

Contents

The present situation   4

What is acid rain?   6

Measuring acid rain   8

What causes acid rain?   10

Effects on nonindustrial areas   12

Threat to human health   14

Threat to forests   16

Threat to water life   18

Threat to agricultural crops   20

Damage to buildings   22

The picture around the world   24

The solution so far   26

What about the future?   28

Further information   30

Glossary   31

Index   32

Words printed in *italic* are explained in the glossary.

Scientific research shows that acid rain has harmed the environment in some places. The word "acid" comes from the Latin "acidus," meaning sour. Foods like lemon juice and vinegar are acids. Acid rain is rain that is more acidic than normal.

Agricultural problems

Most plants have a particular type of environment where they grow best. Farmers grow varieties of plants best suited to the climate and soil in their area. Acid rain can change the *environment,* so the plants do not grow as well. Poor tree growth in some European and American forests was an early sign telling scientists that acid rain was a problem. Acid rain also can change the water in lakes and streams so fish cannot live there.

Damage to trees was one of the first signs of the acid rain problem.

Damage to buildings

Acid rain or acid pollution *erodes*, or wears away, anything made of stone or metal. Bridges and rail lines are weakened and need repairing or replacing earlier than they would without acid rain. The metal bodies of cars and other vehicles rust more quickly, so the vehicles do not last as long. Acid rain falling on stone monuments and buildings erodes them. Detailed carvings become less clear. Eventually, the stone's details disappear unless replaced with new stone.

Acid rain makes vehicles rust quickly.

Poor health

Some acid pollution takes the form of acidic particles in the air. When people breathe in these particles, they damage the lungs. This damage causes asthma and other breathing difficulties and illnesses. For people who already have breathing problems, acid pollution makes them worse and can cause death. As a result, some people are less healthy and need more time off from work and school.

Acid pollution makes breathing problems worse.

◆ How you can help

A clear link exists between acid rain and the fuel used in *industry*. Helping industry use less fuel will reduce acid rain damage. You can help by doing simple things such as walking to school if possible, turning lights out when you leave a room, turning down the heating, and switching off computers when you are finished using them.

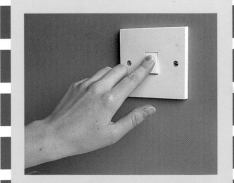

Using less energy could help solve the acid rain problem.

What is acid rain?

The atmosphere makes it possible for water and acid pollution to move around as clouds and rain.

A mixture of gases called the *atmosphere* surrounds the Earth like a blanket. The atmosphere also contains tiny dust particles and polluting gases, which can dissolve in the clouds and fall as rain. If the dissolved gases and particles in the rain have more acid than normal, acid rain results.

How acid rain is caused

Pure water is not an acid, but even clean rainwater is slightly acidic. This acidity results because carbon dioxide from the air has dissolved in the water. Rain is called "acid rain" only if it has more acid than normal. The main causes of acid rain are gases called sulfur dioxide (SO_2) and nitrogen oxides (NO_x). These gases dissolve in the water in the atmosphere to make acids. Bright sunlight speeds up the process, making the acid rain problem worse.

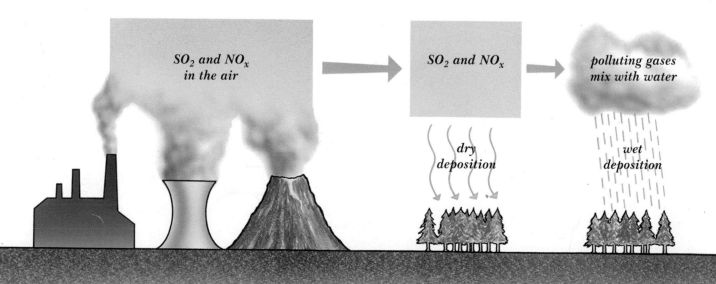

SO_2 and NO_x in the air

SO_2 and NO_x

polluting gases mix with water

dry deposition

wet deposition

Natural acid rain

Although human activities cause most acid rain, some acid rain occurs naturally. Erupting volcanoes emit, or give off, smoke containing water vapor, carbon dioxide, sulfur dioxide, and nitrogen *compounds*. The sulfur dioxide and nitrogen compounds cause small amounts of acid rain near the volcano.

Erupting volcanoes emit gases that cause acid rain.

Acid deposition

Acid deposition occurs when anything acidic falls to the ground from the air. Dry acid deposition, acid gases, and particles make up about half the acid landing on the Earth. Wet acid deposition includes rain, snow, and fog that are more acidic than normal. Acid rain soaks into the ground, making the soil acidic. Dry acid deposition also can make the soil acidic. Blowing wind causes particles and acid gases to land on buildings and vehicles. Later, rainwater washes the particles into the soil.

◆ Sustainable solution

Vehicle exhaust fumes contain large amounts of nitrogen oxides and some sulfur dioxide. Much has been done to reduce these fumes. Since 1983 in the United States and 1993 in Europe, new cars have been fitted with catalytic converters that reduce the amount of nitrogen oxides. Fuel companies have improved fuels so they contain less sulfur and burn more completely. Laws measure and control the amount of harmful gases vehicles may emit.

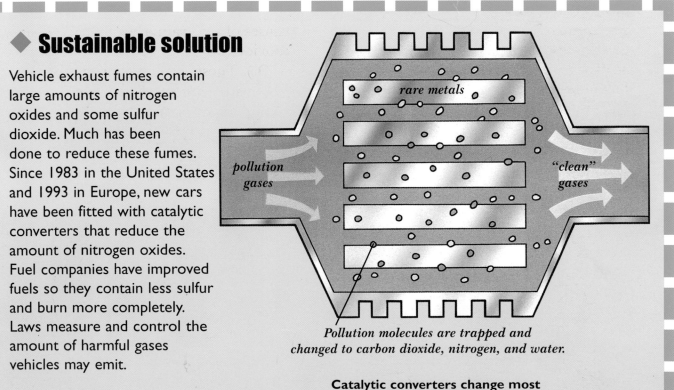

rare metals

pollution gases

"clean" gases

Pollution molecules are trapped and changed to carbon dioxide, nitrogen, and water.

Catalytic converters change most harmful gases into safer ones.

Measuring acid rain

Strong acids can damage a wide range of materials. Scientists can measure the acidity of rain and particles in the air. Measurements help scientists find out where the acid pollution comes from and estimate how much damage it will cause.

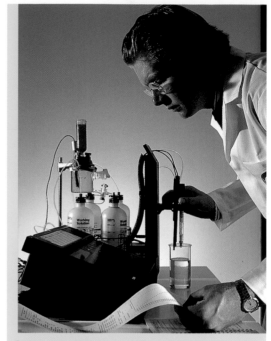

Scientists can use pH meters to measure how acidic the rain is.

Using pH numbers

pH numbers tell scientists how acidic or alkaline something is. Alkaline substances are the opposite of acids. Alkalis can be mixed with acids to neutralize them. A pH of 1 is an extremely strong acid, while 7 is neutral, neither acid nor alkali. A pH of 14 is an extremely strong alkali. Your stomach juices have a pH of about 1.05–2.0, lemon juice 2.3, clean rainwater about 6.5, blood 7.4, and toothpaste 9.9. Acid rain is usually defined as rainwater with a pH of 5.5 or lower. The pH level can be measured with *indicator solutions* that change color when put into different strength of acids and alkalis. Scientists use pH meters.

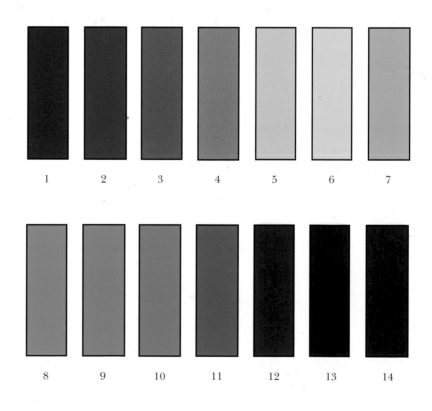

The color of the indicator solution tells how acidic a substance is.

Measuring atmospheric acidity

Scientists measure dry acid pollution by collecting air samples and testing them for a range of harmful chemicals. The scientists compare the number of chemical molecules with the number of air molecules. The values are given as parts per million (ppm). That is the number of pollution molecules in one million air molecules. Scientists also collect samples of rainwater and measure its acidity using a pH meter or indicator.

Limestone and chalk rocks are naturally alkaline. They neutralize the effects of acid rain.

Air quality monitoring stations collect air samples to check for polluting gases and other substances.

Measuring the acidity of soil

When acid rain soaks into soil, the soil becomes acidic. You can buy simple testing kits that measure the soil's acidity by mixing a small amount of soil with an indicator solution and observing the color change. The rocks making up the soil, as well as the rain falling on it, affect the acidity of soil. Soils that contain limestone rock are naturally alkaline. The alkaline rocks in these soils neutralize acid rain falling on the soil.

◆ Science in action

Collect rainwater samples from different places in your area. Use universal indicator paper, available from your school or from chemistry sets, to measure the acidity of the different samples. How acidic is the rain? Does it vary in different local places? If it does, can you suggest any reasons why?

What causes acid rain?

All activities that burn fossil fuel cause some acid rain.

Burning fuel causes acid rain. Most of today's fuels are *fossil fuels* formed from plants and animals that died millions of years ago. Many fossil fuels release sulfur dioxide and nitrogen oxides when they are burned, and these gases cause acid rain. Several factors affect the amount of acid rain, such as the type of fossil fuel used and how completely it is burned.

The history of acid rain

Acid rain began with the Industrial Revolution in Europe about 1750, when steam power began to be used to drive machinery. Large amounts of fossil fuels were burned to create energy. The problem of acid rain became gradually worse, until, in the late 20th century, scientists began to observe widespread *environmental damage*. Since the acid rain problem was discovered, scientists have tried several changes to prevent more damage to the environment and undo existing damage.

The problem of acid rain began with chimneys like these in the Industrial Revolution of 1750.

Industry and cars

Scientists have blamed power stations, furnaces, and motor vehicles for causing acid rain. U.S. studies show that industrial and home furnaces and boilers, as well as power stations that burn fossil fuels, produce more than two-thirds of the sulfur dioxide and half of the nitrogen oxides in the atmosphere. Motor vehicles using gasoline or diesel fuel produce most of the remaining nitrogen oxides.

Coal-burning industries produce most of the sulfur dioxide.

Scientific research

The chemical reactions that take place in the atmosphere to produce acid rain are complicated. At first, many industries argued there was no proof they were to blame for acid rain. Governments tended to agree with the industries, because it was expensive to reduce the amount of pollution. But since the 1980s, governments and industries have worked together to introduce laws to reduce *emissions* that cause acid rain.

Politicians play an important part in reducing the emissions that cause acid rain.

◆Sustainable solution

Power stations reduce sulfur dioxide emissions by using cleaner coal containing less sulfur and emitting less sulfur dioxide than other coals when it burns. Devices called scrubbers are fitted to chimneys to chemically remove sulfur dioxide from the waste gases. Some power stations are changing to natural gas, which creates only tiny amounts of sulfur dioxide. Others use non-fossil fuel technologies, such as hydroelectric power, solar power, or other nonfossil fuel technologies that produce no sulfur dioxide at all.

Using wind power to generate electricity does not cause acid rain.

Industrial activity and vehicle exhaust cause most acid rain. But acid rain affects more than just industrial areas. Many of the most affected areas are *rural areas* hundreds of miles from any industry.

Some areas most affected by acid rain are many miles from industrial areas.

How acid rain gases move around

Smoke particles are heavier than air. They usually sink to Earth near their source. The gases and particles that cause acid rain are much lighter. Air currents carry them long distances. In low wind speeds or weather conditions that prevent warm air from rising, the polluting gases and particles stay near their source, causing problems there. In higher wind speeds, the gases can travel hundreds of miles.

The purpose of tall chimneys

Industry has used tall chimneys since before people knew about acid rain. Tall chimneys release smoke high into the atmosphere. By the time the smoke sinks to the ground, it has spread over a large area. Because the smoke at ground level has thinned out so much, visibility and smells are improved, causing fewer human breathing problems.

Polluting gases spread much farther from their source in high wind speeds.

rainwater with
high acidity

rainwater with
medium acidity

prevailing wind

Prevailing winds can
carry acid rain
hundreds of miles from
where it was created.

Where does the acid rain go?

Prevailing winds are regular patterns of airflow around the Earth. This means most acid rain moves predictably from its source to the area where it falls. Many forests in Central Europe have had acid rain damage partly because of the activities of neighboring countries. Canadian scientists estimate about half the sulfur deposited as acid rain in Canada comes from U.S. sources.

Science in action

Water currents and air currents behave the same way. You can use currents in water to show the effect that air temperature has on polluting gases.

You will need a glass, hot water, cold water, food coloring, 2 clear jars, and a drinking straw.

In a glass, carefully mix 3 drops of food coloring in hot water. This is your "pollution." Fill 2 clear jars, one with hot water and the other with cold water. Dip the drinking straw in the "pollution" to fill the straw and place your finger over the opposite end. Keeping that end of the straw sealed, release a small amount of "pollution" slowly into the bottom of each jar. Does the "pollution" move the same way in each jar?

Threat to human health

Acid deposition can be in the form of dry acidic gases and particles in the air. All animals, including humans, breathe in these particles when they breathe polluted air. The damage caused depends on how many harmful particles are in the air.

Here the air pollution is obvious, but many harmful particles in the air are invisible.

Acid particles inside the lungs can cause serious breathing problems or even death.

The effects of breathing acid pollution

Sulfur dioxide and nitrogen oxide gases mix with oxygen, water, and chemicals in the atmosphere. These mixed gases form tiny acidic particles that are inhaled deep into the lungs. This makes the inside of the lungs sore and causes illnesses such as bronchitis and asthma. In extreme cases, people can die from these lung illnesses and related problems, such as heart disease.

Temperature inversions

The atmosphere usually gets colder farther above the Earth's surface. Warm air at ground level usually rises, taking air pollution with it. *Temperature inversions* occur when a layer of warmer air higher up covers the warm air at ground level. In temperature inversions, the *smog,* a mixture of fog and pollution, is trapped near the ground. In cities such as Mexico City and Tokyo, some people die from breathing problems during temperature inversions.

These children are helping solve the problem of acid rain by walking to school safely with an adult instead of riding in cars or buses.

◆ **How you can help**

Much of the acid pollution in towns comes from vehicle emissions. You can help reduce this pollution by using public transportation instead of cars whenever possible. Walking or riding a bicycle is even better, since these activities produce no pollution. Some schools organize "walking buses" so groups of children can walk to school safely with an adult.

Pollution in different areas

The threat to human health is greatest in areas with the highest number of particles of acid pollution in the air. This is usually in areas with fossil-fuel burning industries or busy traffic. Research shows that children living near major roads are more likely to have asthma than children in rural areas. One difficulty scientists have is that other air pollutants can cause similar illnesses to acid pollution. Scientists have to work out how much illness the acid pollution causes.

Looking like a layer of fog, pollution seems to float over some cities.

Threat to forests

In 1984, reports said acid rain had damaged almost half the trees in the Black Forest in Germany. Other studies soon reported similar damage in areas of the northern United States, Canada, and northern Europe.

Forest damage

For years, scientists had observed that forests in some areas grew more slowly than expected. Tree leaves or needles turned brown and fell off, while some trees died completely. Tests of the air, soil, and water showed that what all these areas had in common was acid rain.

How acid rain affects forests

Acid rain weakens trees by soaking into the soil. As soil becomes more acidic, rain dissolves and washes away *nutrients* from the soil. Sometimes, the soil releases *toxic substances*. Tree roots grow weaker, making them more likely to be damaged by disease, wind, and cold weather.

The trees in this New York forest have lost needles and branches and are dying because of the effects of acid rain.

Acid rain and high altitudes

The same amount of acid rain damages trees at *high altitudes* more than trees on lower ground. Scientists believe this is because clouds of acidic fog often surround trees at high altitude. This fog removes nutrients from the needles or leaves. Trees become weaker and are more likely to be killed by the colder temperatures found at high altitudes.

Trees stop growing naturally at very high altitudes. Acid rain stops trees from growing at lower altitudes.

What areas are most affected?

Trees growing in some places seem able to survive acid rain better than trees in other places. This difference is because the amount of damage caused depends on the type of soil and the amount of acid rain. If the soil is naturally acidic, the extra acidity of acid rain can be just enough to harm the trees. Trees in areas with thin soils also suffer more, because that soil makes it harder for these trees to grow. Acid rain can be the extra problem that makes growth impossible.

Some soils contain chalk or limestone that prevents the acid rain from causing too much damage.

◆ How you can help

The forests damaged most are those where the trees are exposed to other problems along with acid rain. By buying wood products with a Forest Stewardship Council (FSC) label, you are buying wood from trees grown in healthy forests, allowing forest environments damaged by acid rain time to recover.

FSC ©

Threat to water life

The beautiful, clear blue color of this Norwegian lake shows that few plants or animals live in the water because of acid rain damage.

Lakes and streams become acidic when acid rain falls on them. The drainage of acid rain through surrounding soils causes additional damage. Acid rain can also dissolve toxic chemicals from the soil and wash them into rivers and streams.

Acid lakes

Most freshwater lakes and streams have a natural pH between 6 and 8. In June 2001, the United States Environmental Protection Agency (EPA) reported that the pH level in some North American lakes was below 5. In one case, the pH was as low as 4.2. In many freshwater lakes in Norway and Sweden, aluminum released from surrounding acidic soil has poisoned whole fish populations and other *aquatic life*. Many lakes and streams in mountain areas become acidic during storms and in spring. This is because the lakes are filled by heavy rain or melting snow draining from surrounding hills.

Effect on aquatic environments

Even when fish and aquatic insects survive the acidity and toxic chemicals acid rain washes from the soil, the animals' growth is often affected. Adults are smaller, more likely to die from disease, and less likely to reproduce successfully. Even if they do reproduce, their young are more vulnerable to the acid than are adults. Most fish eggs will not hatch in water with a pH of 5 or lower. Animals that eat these fish and insects also suffer as their food disappears.

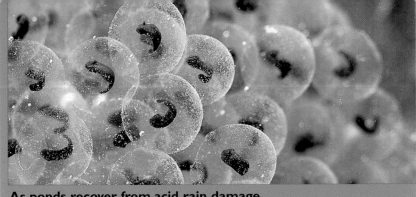

As ponds recover from acid rain damage, more frog young are likely to survive.

Recovering from acid rain damage

If acid rain that poisons lakes and streams is removed, water systems do recover. In 1999, U.S. scientists reported that lakes and streams across the United States and Europe appeared to be getting less acidic. But they warned it would be decades before all the damage was undone.

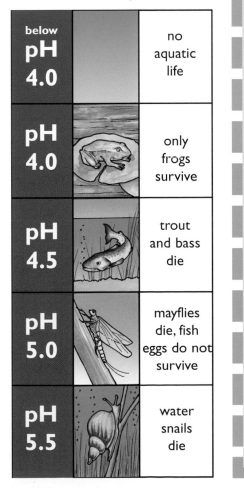

below pH 4.0		no aquatic life
pH 4.0		only frogs survive
pH 4.5		trout and bass die
pH 5.0		mayflies die, fish eggs do not survive
pH 5.5		water snails die

◆ Nonsustainable solution

Acids are neutralized, or prevented from working, by mixing them with alkalis. Limestone is a naturally occurring alkali. In some of the most affected areas, limestone is added to lakes to make them less acidic, allowing fish and other aquatic life to survive. This is a short-term, nonsustainable solution. It is expensive and has to be repeated to prevent the water from becoming acidic again. Adding limestone is not an alternative to addressing the cause of the problem.

Adding limestone to lakes neutralizes some of the acid, but this procedure is expensive.

Acid rain harms many plants, not just trees. While rain that is very acidic can slow the growth of plant leaves, acid rain soaking into the soil causes the most damage. How well plants survive depends on the plant, and more importantly, on whether the acidity stays in the soil. Sometimes, the acidity drains away or the soil itself neutralizes the acid.

Acid rain on leaves

When acid rain falls on plants, it damages the waxy outer coating of their leaves. This damages the leaf's protection against disease, making the plant more likely to be damaged by fungi. Acid rain damages leaves in midgrowth more than young leaves or old leaves. Damage to the outer coating of leaves also can block the *stomata*. These are the holes that allow the leaf to absorb carbon dioxide. When the stomata are blocked, the leaf is unable to create food for itself as rapidly, reducing the amount of food available to the rest of the plant.

stomata let gases in and out

veins

If the outer covering of the leaf is damaged, the plant loses most of its protection against disease.

Coping with the effects of acid rain

Farmers can prevent many damaging effects of acid rain. They treat *agricultural crops* with lime and other chemicals to neutralize the acid and with fertilizers to replace the nutrients acid rain dissolves from the soil. Farmers also can grow varieties of crops that are better able to cope with more acidic soil.

Farmers can often use chemicals or fertilizers to reduce damage caused by acid rain.

Some plants such as cotton grass survive well in acidic soils.

Acid soil

Acid rain causes soil to become more acidic than normal. Most plants tolerate a range of acidity, but soil that is too acidic weakens the roots, so the whole plant is weakened and harvests are smaller. Seeds do not grow as well in more acidic soils, so the plant does not reproduce successfully.

◆ **Science in action**

You will need 3 trays of seedlings, distilled water, and vinegar.

The most acidic rain has about the same pH value as vinegar. Take 3 identical trays of healthy seedlings, such as grass. For one week, water one tray with distilled water, one tray with an equal mix of vinegar and distilled water, and one tray with vinegar. Give the same amount of liquid to each of the trays every day. Do all the plants grow equally well? If not, which seem healthier?

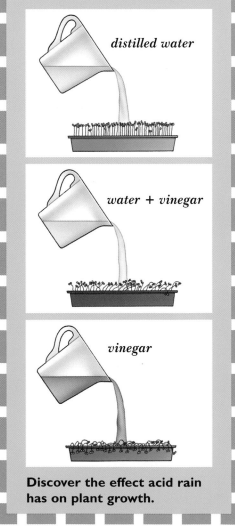

distilled water

water + vinegar

vinegar

Discover the effect acid rain has on plant growth.

Acid rain damages stonework and makes decorative carvings hard to see.

Acid rain affects everything it falls on, not just vegetation. Many buildings and materials show acid rain damage. Just as with human health, forests, water life, and crops, the more acidic the rain, the more damage it causes.

Acid rain on stonework

Clean rain running down stonework causes some slow erosion, called weathering. When acidic rain falls on marble or limestone, the weathering appears to happen much more quickly. This quick weathering is because marble and limestone are alkaline rocks that react with the acidic rain, making it less acidic by "using up" some of the stone. Many stone statues and decorative carvings on buildings are made of marble or limestone because these types of stone are beautiful and easy to work with. Dry acid deposition also damages stonework such as the Egyptian pyramids.

Dry acid deposition has damaged this ancient stonework at the base of the pyramids in Giza, Egypt.

Acid rain on metal

Steel and iron rust when they get damp. Rust is a type of *corrosion*. Most common metals used in construction corrode when they get damp. Acid rain makes the corrosion happen faster, because the metal reacts with the acid to produce rust. Bridges, railroad lines, and all other metal structures exposed to acid rain are weakened and have to be repaired more often than if the rain were less acidic.

Acid rain corrodes metal structures more quickly than rain that is not so acidic.

Protection from acid rain

Most metals exposed to rain are painted to prevent corrosion. The paint protects the metal itself, but the acid rain damages the paint instead. Structures exposed to acid rain have to be repainted more often than if the rain were clean. Paint often cannot be used to protect decorative stonework. Old stone just has to be replaced with new stone when it becomes too eroded.

Car manufacturers use acid-resistant paint for new vehicles.

◆ Science in action

You will need 4 small glass jars, distilled water, white vinegar, 2 pieces of chalk, and 2 pennies.

Fill 2 of the containers with distilled water and the other 2 containers with white vinegar. Place the chalk in one container of vinegar and a clean, shiny penny in the other. Place the second penny and the other piece of chalk in the containers of water. Leave them for 48 hours. What do you observe? Can you explain what has happened?

penny in water

chalk in water

penny in vinegar

chalk in vinegar

The amount of acid pollution varies around the world. Some countries produce much more acid rain than others. Patterns of industrial activity, prevailing winds, climates, and soil types mean different countries suffer different amounts of acid rain damage.

The areas shown in red are places that produce the most acid rain pollution.

The areas shown in blue are places scientists know have been harmed by acid rain.

Which areas of the world are most affected?

The exact effect of acid rain worldwide is not easy to know because scientists have studied some areas more than others. In areas scientists have studied, they have found widespread effects.

• In 1984, almost half the trees in some Central European forests showed acid rain damage.

• The soils in large areas of the northeastern United States are so damaged they lower productivity of forestry, fisheries, and agriculture.

• In 2001, Environment Canada's website reported more than 80 percent of Canadians live in areas with high acid-rain pollution. Damage from acid rain may cost $1 billion a year in Canada.

• Scientists believe acid rain damaged 40 percent of China during its rapid industrial growth of the 1990s.

• Acid rain damage seriously threatens human health and agriculture in about 15 percent of the former Soviet Union.

International cooperation

In the 1970s, scientists began studying the problem of acid rain. They quickly realized it was not just one country's problem. The countries most affected by acid rain were not always the countries causing the problems. Scientists from different countries share their research results with each other.

Beginning to find solutions has taken a long time. Scientists have had to find out exactly what environmental damage acid rain causes and what damage is caused by something else. Politicians have had to find solutions that work and that share the cost fairly among different countries.

Scientists around the world work together to solve the problem of acid rain.

◆ How you can help

Choose items carefully when you go shopping. Much fuel is used to make unnecessary plastic packaging. By buying articles with only the packaging they need, you will be solving environmental problems and saving money. When buying large items like washing machines or cars, ask your family to find out which ones use the least energy or the cleanest fuel.

Buying products without unnecessary wrapping helps save energy.

Attempts to limit and repair the damage from acid rain started in the late 1970s and early 1980s. Scientists expect that without these attempts, the problem of acid rain would worsen by as much as 50 percent in the next 50 years. Efforts have concentrated on controlling and reducing the two main causes of acid rain: sulfur dioxide and nitrogen oxides.

Controlling nitrogen oxides

Governments have concentrated on controlling the amount of nitrogen oxides emitted by motor vehicles. All gasoline and diesel engines emit some nitrogen oxides, but old or badly maintained engines emit the most. Since the 1980s and 1990s, some cities require vehicles to be tested every year and have limited the amount of nitrogen oxides vehicles may emit. Vehicles that emit too much fail the test. The vehicles must be improved before they can be driven again.

Emission tests measure the amount of polluting gases vehicles emit.

Controlling sulfur dioxide

Most sulfur dioxide comes from burning coal. Sulfur is present in coal as an impurity, an unneeded extra part that does not burn. When coal is burned, it emits sulfur, which reacts with the air to form sulfur dioxide.

There are three ways to control the amount of sulfur dioxide in the atmosphere. First, power stations can burn coal with less sulfur. Second, scrubbers can be fitted to power stations. Scrubbers chemically remove sulfur from waste gases. Finally, power stations can be built that use a different fuel, often natural gas. But this is only a short-term solution. Some estimates say natural gas supplies will last only 30 or 40 years. The best long-term solution is nuclear power.

◆ Sustainable solution

Since the 1980s, European and U.S. governments have passed laws to control the production of sulfur dioxide and nitrogen oxide. Scientists continue to monitor the activities that produce these gases. Scientists also research ways of reducing them further. Scientists monitor the effect of acid rain on the environment and advise governments about the effectiveness of existing laws and whether they need changing.

Nuclear power stations do not burn coal, so they do not add to the problem of acid rain. But nuclear energy produces waste that is dangerous in other ways.

Everyone can help reduce the acid rain problem. Well-insulated houses take less energy to heat.

Acid rain has damaged many places. But in the last 20 years, the situation has improved in many areas. Whether the problem of acid rain can be solved completely and the damage undone depends on what governments and industries do. Individuals also can help if they choose wisely about the things they buy and do.

Alternative energy

Some energy sources do not burn fossil fuels. The *alternative energy sources* that would solve the acid rain problem include nuclear power, solar power, hydroelectric power, geothermal power, and wind power. At one time, most of these alternative sources were more expensive than fossil fuels. But the cost of wind power has fallen below the cost of fossil fuels.

Hydroelectric power and other alternative energy sources do not cause acid rain.

Acid rain and global warming

Some scientists recently reported that attempts to reduce acid rain may worsen global warming, the gradual warming of the Earth. Global warming occurs when extra carbon dioxide in the atmosphere stops Earth's heat from returning to space. Sulfur dioxide and nitrogen oxides may actually reflect some of the Sun's energy into space, helping slow the rate of global warming. Other scientists are not sure if this is true or what to do about it if it is. More research may provide answers.

Atmospheric pollution reflecting some of the Sun's energy into space

Some scientists believe acid pollution may help prevent global warming.

◆ How you can help

Reducing the amount of fossil fuel industry burns reduces the emission of gases that cause acid rain. Help reduce acid rain by recycling glass, paper, aluminum, steel, and other garbage. Recycling these materials uses less fossil fuel than does making new supplies from raw materials.

Every time you recycle your garbage, you help reduce the amount of acid rain.

Government action

The U.S. Environmental Protection Agency (EPA) has an Acid Rain Program (ARP) that aims to steadily lower sulfur dioxide and nitrogen oxide emissions. The EPA estimates that by 2010, when the ARP reductions are in place, $50 billion a year will be saved from the decrease in health care expenses alone. Many countries worldwide have agreed to new laws, meaning that in 2010, these countries will emit less than half the sulfur dioxide and nitrogen oxides they did in 1980.

Further information

These are websites you can use to learn more about topics mentioned in this book.

The "Learn.co.uk" website from *The Guardian* newspaper has links to other websites that teachers and students may find interesting. It can be found at **www.learn.co.uk/primary/environment**

The Environment Canada website **www.ec.gc.ca/acidrain** is easy to use. It has a "Kids' Corner" explaining acid rain in a clear and simple manner.

The site **www.soton.ac.uk/~engenvir/environment/air/acid.home.html** gives straightforward information.

More information about the Forest Stewardship Council can be found at **http://fscus.org**

www.globalwarming.com is the website of an environmental protection group dedicated to saving the Earth's natural resources and ending environmental pollution.

The U.S. Environmental Protection Agency website **www.epa.gov/airmarkets/acidrain** has information on the causes and effects of acid rain, and on measuring and reducing it. The site also has science experiments and learning activities.

For general environmental information, you can visit the Greenpeace website at **www.greenpeaceusa.org**

Glossary

Acid deposition
The scientific name for acid rain. Wet acid deposition is acidic rain, snow, or fog. Dry acid deposition is dry particles and gases.

Agricultural crops
Plants grown as food for humans or animals.

Alternative energy source
An energy source other than coal, oil, or gas

Aquatic life
Plants or animals that live in rivers, lakes, streams, or other water. The aquatic life affected by acid rain is freshwater life, not sea life.

Atmosphere
A mixture of gases that surrounds the earth.

Compound
Something formed by combining two or more parts.

Corrosion
When water or acid causes chemical changes to a metal. For example, corrosion turns iron into rust.

Emission
A chemical given off by engines or power stations.

Environment
The natural surroundings of an animal or plant.

Environmental damage
Harm to the living things in an area, or harm to the things the living plants and animals need to survive.

Erode
To wear away rock by water or wind. Acid rain erodes rock more quickly than normal rain.

Fossil fuel
Fuel made of the remains of living things from millions of years ago. Coal, oil, and natural gas are all fossil fuels.

High altitude
Area high above sea level.

Indicator solution
A special solution that changes color when mixed with something acidic or alkaline. The solution can tell the levels of acid in soil or rainwater.

Industry
Factories that use machinery to make things, or power stations that make electricity. Most industries use fossil fuels or electricity made from fossil fuels.

Nutrient
A tiny amount of chemicals plants need as food.

pH number
A number that tells scientists the strength of an acid or alkali. A strong acid has a low pH number. Something with pH number 7 is not acid or alkali, but neutral.

Prevailing wind
A regular pattern of airflow around the Earth.

Rural area
An area that is mostly farms or unused countryside, with few towns or industries.

Smog
A mixture of smoke and fog.

Stomata
Holes that allow a leaf to absorb carbon dioxide.

Temperature inversion
A weather pattern where the warm air near the Earth is trapped under a slightly warmer air layer.

Toxic substance
A chemical or material that is poisonous to plants or animals. A substance that is toxic to some living things may be harmless to others.

Index

acid deposition 6, 7, 14, 22

agricultural crops 4, 20–21, 24

air currents 12, 13

alternative energy 11, 28

altitudes 14, 17

aquatic environments 18–19

atmosphere 6, 9, 11, 12, 14, 29

breathing problems 5, 12, 14, 15

buildings 4, 7, 22

carbon dioxide 7, 20, 29

catalytic converter 7

Egyptian pyramids 22

energy saving 5, 25, 28

farmers 4, 21

fertilizers 21

fish 4, 18, 19

food supply 19, 21

Forest Stewardship Council 17

forests 4, 13, 16–17, 24

fossil fuels 10, 11, 15, 27,
        28, 29

global warming 29

human health 5, 12, 14–15, 24, 29

indicators 8, 9

lakes 4, 18–19, 24

laws 11, 26, 27, 29

leaves 20

limestone 9, 17, 19, 22

metal 4, 23

natural acid rain 7

nitrogen oxide 6, 7, 10, 11, 14,
        26, 27, 29

nutrients 16, 17

painting 23

pH numbers 8, 18, 19, 21

power stations 11, 27

recycling 29

rural areas 12

soil 4, 7, 9, 16, 17, 18, 19, 20,
        21, 24

stonework 4, 22, 23

sulfur dioxide 6, 7, 10, 11, 13,
        14, 26, 27, 29

temperature inversion 14

toxic substances 16, 18

universal indicator paper 9

vehicles 4, 7, 11, 12, 15, 23, 25,26

walking buses 15

weathering 22

wind 11, 12, 13, 16, 24, 28